Norb

Did you know this book is ANIMATED?!

Vooks brings storybooks to life and helps inspire a lifelong love of reading.

Download the Vooks app for more!

SCAN CODE TO WATCH!

Written and illustrated by Jonathan Sundy

ISBN 978-0-9984794-0-8   www.vooks.com

Where are you?

by Jonathan Sundy

an Iz + Norb book

Where are you?

Where are you?

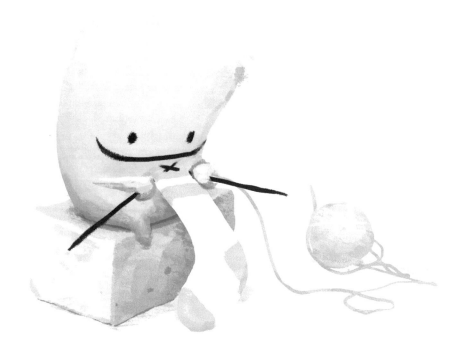

Where are you?

Where are you?

Where are you?

Where are you?

Where are you?

A wee bit LOOPH?
Where are you, goof?

I'm here in this box, safe from hard knocks.

If the HERE where you are isn't the WHERE that you want, don't sit where you are feeling glum on your bum. Get up and start working to change where you're from.

Iz? Where are you?

The end.

Jonathan Sundy is an author, illustrator and art director. His online shop, Jolly Good Gang, offers original art prints, kids books and silly gifts. He attended Notre Dame and lives in beautiful Bend, OR with his wife and two kids.

jsundy@gmail.com | jollygoodgang.com

Printed in the USA
CPSIA information can be obtained
at www.ICGtesting.com
LVHW072243250924
792182LV00012B/43